LINDA McCARTNEY

RETROSPECTIVE
HIGHLIGHTS

INTRODUCTION

Linda McCartney is known for her enticing, intimate portraits of sixties music icons and for being a pioneer of vegetarian cookery: two distinctive elements that bookend her multiple other careers as musician, entrepreneur and animal-rights activist. The *Linda McCartney Retrospective* brings to light her photographic achievements in the decades between capturing the pop culture of the 1960s and starting her vegetarian food brand in the 1990s, before her untimely death in 1998. Like many other female artists before her such as Lee Krasner, Tina Modotti and Dorothea Tanning, Linda's own distinct visual style and accomplishments have been in some ways overshadowed by the huge success of her romantic partner and husband. To address this, the McCartney family have curated the *Retrospective* to act as a true testament to Linda's photographic career, celebrating her as a photographer in her own right who had a keen eye for the unique, the unusual and the humorous in the everyday.

The exhibition has been curated by those who saw at first hand the development of Linda's photographic practice and ambitions over a thirty-year period: her husband Paul and daughters Mary (who also assisted Linda and is herself a renowned contemporary photographer) and Stella (an international fashion designer). Selecting the exhibition from Linda's vast archive, which contains over half a million photographs, prints and memorabilia, the family have encapsulated Linda's wide-ranging themes, from musical legends to nature, family life and social commentary. The photographs also demonstrate Linda's refusal to shy away from the domestic and the everyday – a feature that is one of her most significant contributions to the photographic canon, and yet arguably is also one of the reasons she is often overlooked as a photographer of significance working in the twentieth century.

Throughout art history the 'domestic' – home life, children, cooking and crafts – has often been regarded as trivial when compared to historical paintings, great landscapes or poignant portraits. But for hundreds of years it was the world we were limited to and where women produced much significant art – to paraphrase Virginia Woolf, women artists were often Anonymous. The domestic in Linda's work is most prominent in the seventies and eighties when she was raising a family of four children and did not have the freedom to engage with social commentary or photograph the world's biggest musical stars. Instead, she turned to her surroundings – life on a farm, her ever amusing and growing children, her horses, plants and fun-loving family – to inspire her and act as her subjects. Mary McCartney explains that her mother was overtly interested in photographing normal, banal everyday moments: people brushing their teeth or sitting at the kitchen table.

Linda's first photographs, taken in the early sixties in Tucson, Arizona, were mainly of her horse and her daughter Heather. In 1982 she explained, 'Sitting on a horse's back is a great way for me to see and feel my environment – I take photos while riding and often out of car windows.' In *On Horseback* (Scotland, 1986), the viewer feels they are themselves in the Scottish countryside seeing the beauty of the open landscape, precisely how Linda would have viewed it. The horse's ears and mane bring texture and familiarity to the image. The photograph conveys Linda's mastery of natural light; she particularly loved Scotland for this: 'The light in Scotland is the best light in the world for me. The incredible beauty in old rocks and moss. The sky, the changes in weather. It's good. Good enough for me.'

We can also see Linda's ability to capture natural light in *Lucky Spot in Daisy Field* (Sussex, 1985). Here the horse is presented in a mystical manner: there are no clear tracks of its journey to the middle of the daisies; it is standing freely of its own apparent accord, as if she stumbled upon this horse who appears to be in deep thought. When you learn that Linda took the photograph on a large-format 8x10 camera, you gain a further understanding of who she was as a photographer. Not only did she carry the heavy camera, most likely on a tripod, to the middle of the field, like the intrepid photographers of the late nineteenth century before her, she also managed to get the horse to stand still for her shot. Linda had to trust her instinct that she had got the image she wanted: there is no way to click through multiple frames on an 8x10 camera, and the horse could have moved at any moment. Linda was fond of saying that her approach relied on intuition:

I think you just feel instinctively, you got to just click on the moment. Not before it and not after it. I think if you are worried about light meters and all that stuff, you just miss it. For me it just came from my inners, as they say. Just excitement. I love it – I get very excited.

Linda's facility to quickly see an intriguing composition, strong colours, light and the overall visuality of the image can be credited to an artistic sensibility developed during her upbringing. Her father, Lee Eastman, was a New York lawyer and had a great appreciation of painters and paintings, with some of the twentieth century's most renowned artists becoming his clients. This early introduction to the works of Willem de Kooning and other abstract expressionists trained Linda's eye from a young age. She also credited her summers as a child spent by the sea as another influence on her 'visual eye'. *Family of Man*, curated by Edward Steichen at MoMA, New York, in 1955, was the first photography exhibition to really have an impact on Linda, when she saw it at fourteen years old.

As with photographers such as Ansel Adams or William Eggleston, a lack of formal training did not stop Linda from achieving well-composed, distinctive and magnetic pictures. Despite her father's wish that she train under a professional, Linda did not have the patience for it and wanted to use her instinct instead. Ironically, while this enabled Linda to take the shot of Lucky Spot, there is a sense of patience, respect and knowledge of the medium — and the spirit of the animal — that contributes to the photograph's poeticism. Linda regarded her innocence of formal training as a resource in itself:

I prefer to work by trial and error because some of my best pictures have come precisely because I didn't know enough. By having the 'wrong' setting I've actually come up with something good. This is why I empathise so much with John Lennon, Paul McCartney and Bob Dylan, none of whom read or write music. It's the innocence that's important to them.

The training that Linda did receive extended to two photography classes she took in the early 1960s at the local arts centre in Tucson, Arizona, with Hazel Archer, a teacher who studied at Black Mountain College under Josef Albers and went on to train many significant artists, including Robert Rauschenberg. Here Linda was introduced to the work of Walker Evans, Ansel Adams and Dorothea Lange, which had a profound effect on her. This was the first time she properly focused on black-and-white stills photography. Yet she stated that an interest in cinema from Italy and France developed before this, and that one of the reasons most of her photographs were shot in black and white was the early influence of films such as Fellini's *La Strada* and the Italian neorealism of De Sica's *The Bicycle Thief*; Linda recalled that she 'almost floated out of the cinema after I first saw *La Dolce Vita*'.

Linda described Arizona as one of the most visual states in America, where you could explore the foothills and witness 'sunsets supreme' — somewhere you could become a 'free spirit'. Arizona had a significant impact on Linda as an artist. Not only did she find it visually inspiring, it helped her develop a relaxed approach to image-making and introduced her to photographic greats that she identified with and grew from. Linda explained that she was completely taken by Evans and Lange's photography from the Great Depression:

The photographs of Walker Evans and Dorothea Lange continue to inspire me. They were real artists and showed the character of the people they were dealing with, and even though I went on to photograph a lot of rock and roll musicians I was always more interested in their character than their public image. I wanted to get underneath their skin.

This is evident throughout the *Retrospective*, from the photograph *Mick Jagger* (New York, 1966) to *Eyeglass* (Sussex, 1984). A young Mick Jagger – glancing back at the viewer, framed by curtains drawn as if he is about to walk on stage, looking inquisitive, calm and aware of his surroundings – is a different take to the energised, strutting lead singer he was known for being. In fact, this unguarded shot of Jagger was taken on a boat on the Hudson during the Rolling Stones' first visit to the USA. This glimpse back at Linda, and ultimately the viewer, shows him before he inhabits the persona of 'Mick Jagger'. Linda captured him in an instant. Comparatively, in *Eyeglass* Linda's son James confronts the camera, showing Linda's ability to catch the surreal and beguiling. One magnified eye protrudes in the foreground of the image; there is a sense of 'double looking' – Linda at James and James at his mother. He too has a lens, to observe her with. This is a fun and playful moment between mother and son, and is just as striking a photo as the one of Jagger taken twenty years prior. Additionally,

Eyeglass highlights the quality David Bailey values most about Linda's work:

I once told Linda that she should stop taking photos of Paul and her family and concentrate on other things. I think I was wrong ... I don't know if it is art or not, but I do know that as a social document they are far more important than pictures of the rich and famous.

While working as a photographer for magazines such as *Time*, *Mademoiselle* and *Rolling Stone*, the majority of Linda's pictures were not taken in a studio. The idea of telling people where to stand, what to do and how to pose did not translate to her personal, natural style of photography. Linda explained that she only took photographs when she saw or felt there was something to capture and preferred to 'make a nice day of it' when shooting with someone. Her approach was to enjoy the company of the subject and only to take photographs when a moment arose. This technique – when she was not searching for an image, but instead happened upon a scene and caught its essence – is how her best pictures occurred, whether using her Pentax, her Nikon or her 8x10. We can apply to Linda's work John Berger's idea from *Understanding a Photograph* of the 'special authenticity' found in some photography, whereby the images never suggest the photographer is probing, but rather that they hold an 'offhand' quality, imbued by a caring nonchalance.

One of Linda's early – and continued – achievements was her ability to create decisive and out-of-the-ordinary images from her kind, friendly demeanour, differing from the photographers she cites as influences. Walker Evans famously photographed people on the subway in New York without their knowledge, concealing the camera in his coat. Diane Arbus, another favourite of Linda's, would in her early career continuously take pictures to provoke a reaction to the intrusion.

Linda's skill landed her a job as resident photographer at the Fillmore East in New York. Here she shot the likes of B.B. King and Janis Joplin. It was also Linda's soulful portraits of musicians living and working in New York that raised her profile as a photographer. She was voted the US Female Photographer of the Year in 1967 and became the first ever woman to photograph for the cover of *Rolling Stone* magazine in 1968 with her portrait of Eric Clapton. Linda referred to the sixties as a time with 'hope in the air' and explained that she was unaware of how legendary some of her subjects would become:

It felt like being in Hollywood at the time when Hollywood was relatively innocent. We all knew something was happening but it wasn't discovered yet ... People who later became icons were on the brinks of their careers, wondering whether anybody was ever going to notice them ... That's what made it exciting to be taking photographs.

It was before the self-consciousness set in. I wanted to record what was there – every blemish, every bit of beauty, every emotion. I wasn't interested in manufacturing a show-business image. I would rather photograph a wrinkled apple than a made-up, smooth, glamorous man. Hence the reason I never got into fashion photography.

The sixties laid the foundations for Linda to become a confident photographer, striving for something different and individual. Her contemporaries Garry Winogrand and Lee Friedlander were also shooting the New York of the 1960s; however, compared to her peers, Linda did not approach the city through street photography or the usual scenes of Coney Island or 'man versus skyscraper'. Instead, Linda was at the heart of the New York art scene, alongside Warhol and The Velvet Underground. She showed the essence of the decade's biggest musical stars through her instinctual photos of them on and off stage. The artist Brian Clarke explains that many people try to undermine the importance of Linda's sixties pictures and overlook the fact that others failed to get the photos she did. Clarke compares Linda to Don McCullin and Arbus – also photographers who were in particular places at significant times. McCullin captured the suffering and dying in Vietnam because he was with the suffering and dying in Vietnam. Arbus got the photos of the socially ostracised because she was with the socially ostracised. 'Why do people criticise Linda for getting photos of musicians in the sixties? It was where she was ...'

Linda herself was conscious of this, and in 1976 she cited the shoot she did with Crosby, Stills and Nash in Hampstead, London, in 1969 as a turning-point. Linda was aware at the time that photographing the band somehow felt different. She said the shoot started off well with 'good people and everything was how it ought to be but yet somehow it wasn't as fun or as loose', and it was during this session she realised she had changed. Linda decided it was time for her to take her photographs in the world she loved – the world of her family and Wings.

On tour, Linda captured images while exploring new cities — out of car and bus windows — as well as from the stage during performances with Paul and their band. Yet her ability to find a striking composition and her skilled use of natural light were not compromised. We can see this in 1972's *Girl in a Café*, taken in Copenhagen. A young woman is illuminated by light and framed by a blurred foreground. Linda's focus on the woman presents the idea of time and the 'everyday'. Is this woman patiently waiting for someone? People-watching herself? Or does she have that familiar feeling we can all relate to when in a café or restaurant, hungry and waiting for food? The obscured foreground and a lack of detail of what the other customers are wearing make the image hard to date. This

timeless-looking photograph could have been taken at any moment during Linda's career, but her constant practice at home photographing her own family at the kitchen table helped her capture a moment of intrigue within the ordinary.

By the 1990s, we see Linda reflecting on her photography in a different way again. She admits she took many photos she previously overlooked that were filled with humour or surrealism; photos which are now exhibited in the *Retrospective*. She refers to her photographs as 'stills from a kind of personal road movie recording a slice of my life'. Her life in the nineties meant that Linda's animal-rights activism and passion for spreading the importance of vegetarian eating were now explored through her photography:

If I could get in to a slaughter house I'd show the horrors of life. I'm against animal slaughter and against people eating animals and experimenting on animals and wearing animals ... so photography as a social comment really interests me; it's changed for me now. And I think the social comment thing is more interesting. I think a photograph has to stand on its own without any words.

Lambs' Hearts (Brick Lane, London, 1992) and *Meat Market* (London, 1992) are examples of Linda's refusal to shy away from what she believed in and see her making explicit comment without the need for words to explain her message. *Meat Market* depicts three dead rabbits and a pheasant freshly hanging in a shop. They have not yet been butchered to look like raw meat, their fur and feathers still intact. The white hoods over the rabbits are disturbing and remind us they will soon be beheaded. The focus on the animals and not the customers or surroundings removes all other distractions for the viewer and produces a strong, confrontational message. Linda believed there was a barbarity in the act of killing animals, which is exposed in this unnatural, sterile environment before human consumption.

As well as covering the range of genres and subjects treated by Linda, the *Retrospective* explores the different photographic printing processes she loved and experimented with. Linda was actively engaged with the history of the photographic medium, most prominently in her experiments with 'sun prints' or cyanotypes. The method of making sun prints was invented by William Henry Fox Talbot between 1835 and 1839, with Sir John Herschel pioneering the blue cyanotype in 1840. Paper is coated with a mineral solution and then exposed to natural light rather than the usual method of being developed in a darkroom. Linda had been enticed by the printing quality of old processes in the 1960s when she visited MoMA, stating that they were better than 'anything she had ever seen'. Describing the etched quality of the prints as 'marvellous', Linda wanted to achieve the same effect with her own photos.

Linda stated that the combination of photography and painting had always appealed to her, particularly in the work of Rauschenberg, and looking at her prints such as *Shadow Jumping* (Sussex, 1984) one can see the inspiration. It was with sun prints that Linda found the closest effect she was trying to capture, rather than a mixed-media technique that she had also experimented with. The paint-like quality of *Shadow Jumping* brings the viewer face to face with the hand of the photographer and their involvement in producing the print, from the moment it was captured in the camera to the moment it is presented on the paper. The varying shades of blue echo the shades of colour found in works by the likes of Mark Rothko or the prominent use of blue by Yves Klein. Linda often made six versions of each subject – some printed in blue, some in sepia, some on thick rough art paper, handmade paper and even fabric. She produced a wide spectrum of images – landscapes, still lives, portraits and impromptu images.

One of the aspects of sun-printing that appealed to Linda was that you did not need a darkroom, enlarger or a safety light; you could use a bath – in Linda's case, her daughter's bath – and raw materials, not chemicals. This brought the printing itself back into the realm of the domestic. As well as her 8x10 camera, Linda made sun prints from photos taken on her 35 mm and 2¼-inch cameras – first enlarging the negative to the final size.

This made her sun prints rather different to a nineteenth-century print, possessing a spontaneity that could not be previously achieved due to the long exposure times necessary, which made the clear capturing of movement near impossible.

Polaroids, Polaroid transfers and platinum prints were other techniques Linda explored and mastered. Linda's understanding of light translates well to her Polaroids, which are often filled with rich colours. The surreal and the comical dominate them, and she had an incredible ability to photograph people and things close up and with an immediate crispness. Her Polaroid transfers (when you peel away the negative layer from the Polaroid, press it onto a surface and use the emulsion to create a new image) on the other hand, differ in theme and ambience, and see Linda concentrating on her interest in nature, plants and flowers.

The *Retrospective* is a testament to Linda's photographic range and skill. It shows her ability to capture humour in the everyday, the intimate and poignant portraits of famous faces, the beauty in nature, and the insightful moments that can be caught out of a car window. It illustrates Linda's capacity to tell a story of time, place, people and herself:

I have seen paintings and photographs depicting the horrors of war, the slaughter of animals for human gain and sport, and man's general persecution of his fellow living creatures, be they human or animal. I don't think the world has changed much more because of these visuals, but I do hope they are making the world more aware of the suffering that exists. At the same time, I feel that capturing day-by-day happiness and warmth is also important for a balanced outlook. I am a great believer in the expression 'every picture tells a story'.

Sarah H. Brown
Photographic Curator
Linda McCartney Archive

Linda by Paul.
Scotland, 1970

Opposite: *Linda by Eric Clapton.*

Self Portrait.
Sussex, England, 1992

Self Portrait.
Arizona, 1991

Self Portrait.
Abbey Road Studios, London, 1975

Opposite: *Self Portrait with Paul.*
London, 1970

Judy Collins.
Malibu, California, 1968

Opposite: *Janis Joplin.*
Fillmore East, New York, 1968

John Lennon.
Twickenham Studios, London, 1969

Opposite: *Jimi Hendrix.*
London, 1967

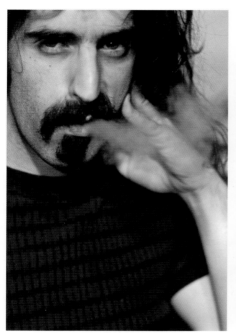

Frank Zappa.
New York, 1968

Charles Aznavour.
Connecticut, 1968

Ginger Baker.
Atlantic Recording Studio,
New York, 1967

Eric Clapton.
London, 1968

Pete Townshend,
Drake Hotel. New York, 1967

Opposite: *Mick Jagger.*
Hudson River, New York, 1966

Sgt. Pepper's Press Launch.
London, 1967

Jimi Hendrix Experience.
London, 1967

The Yardbirds.
London, 1968

Fans.
London, 1979

Opposite: *The Beatles.*
Abbey Road, London, 1969

Twiggy.
London, 1969

Paul.
Los Angeles, 1968

John and Paul.
Abbey Road Studios, London, 1968

Wildman.
South Coast of England, 1969

*Aretha Franklin,
modelling for Mademoiselle.*
Los Angeles, 1968

BB King.
Fillmore East, New York, 1968

John Lennon.
Abbey Road Studios, 1968

Yoko Ono.
London, 1968

Lucky. Sussex, 1976

Opposite: *Snarling Cat.*
Scotland, 1970

Two Romney Sheep.
Sussex, 1987

On Horseback.
Scotland, 1986

Horses in snow.
Sussex, 1986

Stallion's neck.
Standing Stone, Scotland, 1993

Paul, Heather and Ruth on horseback.
Cheshire, 1969

Divided Window.
Sussex, 1985

Mary. Scotland, 1969

Paul and Heather.
London, 1969

Opposite: *Heather.*
Scotland, 1970

Self Portrait with Paul and Mary.
London, 1969

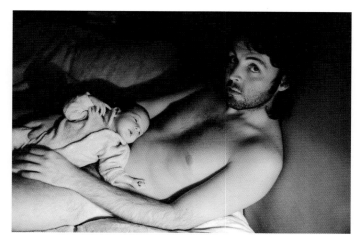

Paul and Mary.
London, 1969

Linda, Paul and Mary.
Cleveland, USA, 1976

James and Martha.
1978

Eyeglass.
Sussex, 1984

James.
London, 1984

Stella.
Tokyo, 1990

Paul.
Jamaica, 1971

Painted Toenails.
Jamaica, 1972

Stella.
Amsterdam, 1989

Mary.
Sussex, 1994

Heavy Load.
New Orleans, 1975

Partial Eclipse.
London, 1984

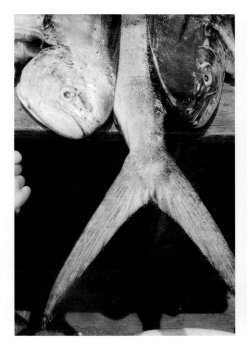 

Dead Fish.
Martinique, 1976

Lambs' Hearts.
Brick Lane, London, 1992

Meat Market.
London, 1992

Portraits.
London, 1977

Girls Peering Through the Gate.
London, 1968

Girl in a Café.
Copenhagen, 1972

Coalmen.
Sussex, 1981

Gilbert and George.
Spitalfields, London, 1985

Women on a Bike.
Portugal, 1968

Glance.
Portugal, 1968

Skis and TV.
USA, 1976

Tracey Ullman.
Elstree Studios, 1982

Allen Ginsberg.
Sussex, 1995

Johnny and Kate.
London, 1995

Mother and Child.
Corfu, 1969

Local Children/Paul and Stella.
Barbados, 1979

Out Here.
California, 1975

Paul, Stella and James.
Scotland, 1982

Opposite: *Mary, Paul and Heather.*
Scotland, 1970

Mary, Paul and Heather.
London, 1969

Paul and Mary.
Scotland, 1969

Paul.
Glasgow, 1970

Paul, Mary and Stella.
Scotland, 1977

Hector.
Scotland, 1970

Man Outside Car.
Scotland, 1968

Local Men.
Campbeltown, Scotland, 1968

Distillery Workers.
Campbeltown, Scotland, 1968

Stallion and Standing Stone.
Scotland, 1996

Opposite: *Polaroids by Linda*

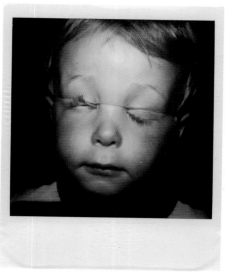

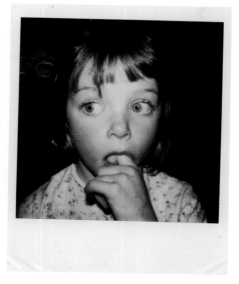

Century.
Portugal, 1968
Polaroid transfer

Winter Rose II.
1980
Polaroid transfer

Stella.
Arizona, 1994
Sun print

Shadow Jumping.
Sussex, 1984
Sun print

Chile Crowd.
The New World Tour, 1993

Self Portrait in Francis Bacon's Studio.
London, 1997